UNDERSTANDING ANXIETY

WHAT IS
SOCIAL ANXIETY?

RACHAEL MORLOCK

PowerKiDS press.

NEW YORK

Published in 2021 by The Rosen Publishing Group, Inc.
29 East 21st Street, New York, NY 10010

First Edition

Editor: Kristen Susienka
Book Design: Rachel Rising

Photo Credits: Cover, p. 17 Africa Studio/Shutterstock.com; Cover, Rawpixel.com/Shutterstock.com; Cover, Matej Kastelic/Shutterstock.com; Cover, Susan Law Cain/Shutterstock.com; Cover, pp. 1, 3,4,56,8,10,12,14,16,18,20,22,23,24 (background) Flas100/Shutterstock.com; Cover, pp. 1,5,7,9,11,13,15,17,19,21 (text box) mhatzapa/Shutterstock.com; p. 4 Ebtikar/Shutterstock.com; p. 5 Iakov Filimonov/Shutterstock.com; p. 6 Kaesler Media/Shutterstock.com; p. 7 Jess Rodrigues/Shutterstock.com; p. 8 ValIza/Shutterstock.com; p. 9 Dragana Gordic/Shutterstock.com; p. 10 Inna Astakhova/Shutterstock.com; p. 11 fizkes/Shutterstock.com; p. 13 Science Photo Library - SCIEPRO/Brand X Pictures/Getty Images; p. 14 leungchopan/Shutterstock.com; p. 15 Nikodash/Shutterstock.com; p. 16 Tamara Kulikova/Shutterstock.com; p. 18 schankz/Shutterstock.com; p. 19 LightField Studios/Shutterstock.com; p. 20 GLRL/Shutterstock.com; p. 21 Brocreative/Shutterstock.com; p. 22 Gelpi/Shutterstock.com.

Some of the images in this book illustrate individuals who are models. The depictions do not imply actual situations or events.

Cataloging-in-Publication Data

Names: Morlock, Rachael.
Title: What is social anxiety? / Rachael Morlock.
Description: New York : PowerKids Press, 2021. | Series: Understanding anxiety | Includes glossary and index.
Identifiers: ISBN 9781725317932 (pbk.) | ISBN 9781725317956 (library bound) | ISBN 9781725317949 (6 pack)
Subjects: LCSH: Anxiety–Juvenile literature. | Anxiety in children–Juvenile literature. | Panic disorders–Treatment–Juvenile literature.
Classification: LCC BF723.A5 M667 2021 | DDC 155.4'18232–dc23–dc23

Manufactured in the United States of America

CPSIA Compliance Information: Batch #CSPK20. For Further Information contact Rosen Publishing, New York, New York at 1-800-237-9932.

Find us on

CONTENTS

WHAT IS SOCIAL ANXIETY? 4

NEGATIVE MESSAGES 6

FEELING ANXIOUS 8

FACING YOUR FEARS 10

WHERE DOES IT COME FROM? 12

TREATING SOCIAL ANXIETY 14

TAKING ON TRIGGERS 16

TOOLS AND TIPS 18

HELPING OTHERS 20

MOVING FORWARD 22

GLOSSARY 23

INDEX 24

WEBSITES 24

WHAT IS SOCIAL ANXIETY?

You feel your face turn red. Your hands are wet with sweat. Your heart pounds in your chest, and your stomach does a flip. Maybe you're standing in front of your class, **performing**, or meeting someone new.

Everyone can think of a time they've felt nervous like this around other people. But some people have these feelings every day. It's called social anxiety. It makes people fear being with others and can make living life hard sometimes.

FEELING NERVOUS AND SHY OFTEN MAKES LIFE HARD. SOCIAL ANXIETY CAN GET IN THE WAY OF MEETING FRIENDS, GOING TO SCHOOL, AND DOING THINGS YOU LOVE.

NEGATIVE MESSAGES

Social anxiety is a strong fear of being watched, being judged, or not being accepted by others. Many people with social anxiety are afraid of **embarrassing** themselves in public. They worry that others will think badly of them because of the things they say or do. Their fear comes from **negative** messages in their mind.

Negative messages can be so loud that they take over other thoughts. They make it hard to feel comfortable and enjoy being with other people.

FEELING ANXIOUS

Fear changes the way you think. It also changes the way your body feels. You might sweat, **blush**, feel shaky, and have trouble speaking. Sometimes, social anxiety makes your heart race. It can make your head or stomach hurt. You might feel dizzy, out of breath, or tired.

Feeling **anxious** can change the way you act. It's common for people with social anxiety to speak too quietly or quickly, stay on the edge of groups, or avoid meeting peoples' eyes.

FACING YOUR FEARS

Fear is natural. It's your body's way of telling you that a **situation** is unsafe. But sometimes your brain makes a mistake—it tells you that a situation is unsafe when it isn't.

When this happens, fear can keep you from doing normal, everyday things for a long time. If fear makes it hard for you to go to school, learn, make friends, or talk to others, then a doctor might tell you that you have social anxiety **disorder**.

WHERE DOES IT COME FROM?

Social anxiety is nothing to be embarrassed about. Lots of people have it. It's usually genetic. That means it's passed down in families. Your life at home and with your parents can lead to social anxiety, too.

Children who are shy might have more social anxiety as they get older. Being bullied or having something frightening happen sometimes leads to social anxiety, too. No matter where it comes from, you can learn to handle social anxiety.

THE PART OF YOUR BRAIN IN CHARGE OF FEAR IS CALLED THE AMYGDALA, SHOWN HERE IN RED. THE WAY THE AMYGDALA WORKS CAUSES SOCIAL ANXIETY.

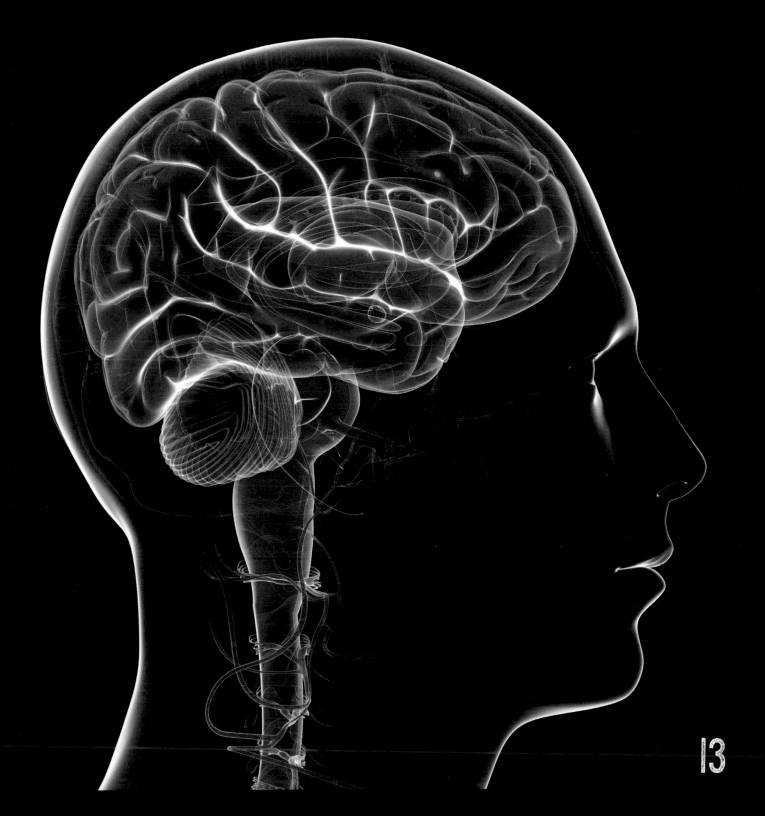

13

TREATING SOCIAL ANXIETY

After a doctor has **diagnosed** a social anxiety disorder, they can help you treat it. Everyone is different, and a doctor will find the best choices for you. **Therapy** is a common tool for treating social anxiety. A therapist listens to your fears. Then they help you safely face them one by one.

Over time, positive messages take the place of negative messages in your mind. Therapy takes trust and **courage**. It can help you build skills and find strength.

TAKING ON TRIGGERS

A therapist helps you understand **triggers** for anxiety. A trigger could be playing a sport or an instrument in public. In school, it might mean giving a report or asking and answering questions. Talking to strangers, going to parties, visiting friends, eating with others, or using public bathrooms can also trigger social anxiety.

A therapist helps you move toward triggers instead of away from them. Each time you do something even though you're afraid, you prove that you can handle anxiety.

AVOIDING TRIGGERS CAN LEAVE YOU FEELING VERY LONELY. IF YOUR FEARS TAKE OVER, YOU END UP MISSING OUT ON FRIENDSHIPS AND FUN.

TOOLS AND TIPS

It's hard to face triggers if your body and mind are filled with fear. Anxiety is often worst while you're waiting for something to happen. To calm anxiety, try deep breathing, **mindfulness**, or body movements like yoga. These practices keep you in the present moment.

If you feel anxiety building up, try walking outside, listening to music, writing in a journal, or making art. For some people, a therapy animal can be a calming companion.

HELPING OTHERS

If a friend or family member has social anxiety, you can help them realize how strong they are. Be there when they're feeling sad or lonely, help them remember their purpose, and cheer for their successes. You can also work together to build social skills. Ask if they'd like to play a game where you pretend to be strangers. Then take turns saying hello, listening, asking questions, meeting their eyes, and joining a group. Practicing this way can be helpful and fun!

BULLYING CAN CAUSE SOCIAL ANXIETY OR MAKE IT WORSE. YOU CAN STAND UP FOR OTHERS WHO ARE BULLIED AND CHOOSE TO BE KIND AND WELCOMING TO EVERYONE YOU MEET.

MOVING FORWARD

Learning about social anxiety is an important step in dealing with it. As you practice facing your fears, you'll realize that you're braver than you thought! Notice the times when you've worked through anxiety to join others or complete a task. Your successes tell you how strong you are and show you that you don't need to be afraid.

In the end, you might find that the friendships you make and the new adventures you have are worth the struggle.

GLOSSARY

anxious: Afraid or nervous.

blush: To turn red because you're upset or ashamed.

courage: Bravery.

diagnose: To figure out what a disease is by looking at the signs.

disorder: A sickness or medical condition.

embarrass: To make someone (including yourself) feel ashamed or ill at ease in front of others.

mindfulness: Paying attention to your thoughts and feelings in the present moment without judging them.

negative: Harmful, bad, or unwanted.

perform: To carry out or do.

situation: Facts, conditions, and events that affect someone at a time and place.

therapy: A way of dealing with problems to make people feel better.

trigger: Something that begins or stirs up a feeling or reply.

INDEX

A

amygdala, 12

B

body, 8, 10, 18
brain, 10, 12
bullying, 21

D

disorder, 10
doctor, 10, 11, 14, 15

F

family, 12, 20
fear, 6, 8, 10, 11, 12, 17, 18, 22
feelings, 4

H

head, 8
heart, 4, 8

M

medicines, 15
mood, 9

N

negative messages, 6, 7, 14

P

public, 6, 16

S

stomach, 4, 8

T

therapist, 14, 16
therapy, 14, 15, 18, 19
thoughts, 6
triggers, 16, 18

WEBSITES

Due to the changing nature of Internet links, PowerKids Press has developed an online list of websites related to the subject of this book. This site is updated regularly. Please use this link to access the list: www.powerkidslinks.com/ua/socialanxiety